MEET JOSH HAMILTON

Baseball's Unbelievable Comeback

Ethan Edwards

PowerKiDS press
New York

Published in 2014 by The Rosen Publishing Group, Inc.
29 East 21st Street, New York, NY 10010

First Edition

Editor: Jennifer Way
Book Design: Greg Tucker
Book Layout: Colleen Bialecki
Photo Research: Katie Stryker

Photo Credits: Cover, p. 7 Paul Spinelli/Stringer/Major League Baseball/Getty Images; pp. 4, 9, 30 David Banks/Contributor/Getty Images Sport/Getty Images; p. 10 © AP Images; pp. 12, 13 Peter Read Miller/Contributor/Sports Illustrated/Getty Images; p. 15 Rick Stewart/Stringer/Hulton Archive/Getty Images; p. 16 Ezra Shaw/Staff/Getty Images Sport/Getty Images; p. 17 Major League Baseball/Contributor/Getty Images; p. 18 Brad Mangin/Contributor/Sports Illustrated/Getty Images; p. 19 Mike Stobe/Stringer/Getty Images Sport/Getty Images; pp. 20, 25, 27 Fort Worth Star Telegram/Contributor/McClatchy Tribune/Getty Images; p. 22 John Grieshop/Stringer/Major League Baseball/Getty Images; p. 24 John Williamson/Contributor/Getty Images Sport/Getty Images; p. 26 Bob Levey/Contributor/Getty Images Sport/Getty Images; p. 28 Thearon W. Henderson/Contributor/Getty Images Sport/Getty Images.

Library of Congress Cataloging-in-Publication Data

Edwards, Ethan.
  Meet Josh Hamilton : baseball's unbelievable comeback / by Ethan Edwards. — 1st ed.
     pages cm. — (All-star players)
  Includes index.
  ISBN 978-1-4777-2914-4 (library binding) — ISBN 978-1-4777-3003-4 (pbk.) —
ISBN 978-1-4777-3074-4 (6-pack)
  1. Hamilton, Josh, 1981-–Juvenile literature. 2. Baseball players–United States–Biography–Juvenile literature. 3. Recovering addicts–United States–Biography–Juvenile literature. I. Title.
  GV865.H24E38 2014
  796.357092–dc23
  [B]
                             2013020937
Manufactured in the United States of America

CPSIA Compliance Information: Batch #W14PK2: For Further Information contact Rosen Publishing, New York, New York at 1-800-237-9932

Contents

Down but Not Out   5

Hammer   6

Minor Leagues   11

Crash   14

The Winning Inning   19

Most Valuable Player   23

Giving Back   26

The Natural   29

Stat Sheet   30

Glossary   31

Index   32

Websites   32

Down but Not Out

It might seem that baseball star Josh Hamilton enjoys an easy life. After all, he is one of the biggest stars and best hitters in Major League Baseball. He was **drafted** right out of high school as one of the best young baseball players in years. There was little doubt that he would be among the very best ballplayers of all time.

Then he almost lost everything. Hamilton has spent years battling an **addiction** to drugs and **alcohol**. His close friends and family have stood by him. Hamilton worked hard to stay clean and return to baseball. Now he is better than ever.

After five years with the Texas Rangers, Josh Hamilton is now an outfielder for the Los Angeles Angels of Anaheim.

Hammer

Josh Hamilton was born in Raleigh, North Carolina, on May 21, 1981. His parents were big baseball fans, and Josh and his brother were great athletes. Josh grew quickly for his age and was especially good at baseball, track, soccer, and football. He eventually decided to concentrate only on baseball. One reason was because he could not find track shoes big enough for his feet! He had to get special baseball shoes, or cleats, made just for him. Josh practiced as much as possible. He knew baseball was in his future.

Before he played baseball professionally, Josh Hamilton won three state championships in a row with his Little League team.

Sportswriter Tim Stevens wrote about Josh's high-school days. He commented, "It was hard to write about him sometimes because it felt like his story was make-believe."

Josh attended Athens Drive High School and played **outfield** and pitched for the Athens Drive Jaguars. He was such a great hitter that his teammates nicknamed him Hammer. He stood 6 feet 4 inches (1.9 m) in high school and weighed 200 pounds (91 kg).

His pitch was timed at more than 90 miles per hour (145 km/h), and he could hit the ball out of the park. He was named North Carolina's Player of the Year for two years in a row and was even on the cover of the magazine *Baseball America* while he was still in high school! There was nothing stopping Josh Hamilton from becoming one of the game's biggest stars.

Hamilton was a powerful hitter from a young age. When he came to bat as a Little Leaguer, infielders moved to the outfield!

Minor Leagues

Top baseball scouts watched Josh Hamilton's high-school baseball career, and they liked what they saw. In 1999, the Tampa Bay Devil Rays were a new team that had played only a single season. This meant they got the first pick in the draft, and they picked Josh Hamilton. Unlike athletes in other professional sports, baseball players are not ready for the top level as soon as they enter the draft. Baseball players need to work on their game in the minor leagues. It can take several years, but the best minor-league players usually make it to the majors, or Major League Baseball.

In 2000, USA Today named Josh Hamilton the Minor League Player of the Year. The award is given to the minor-league player who had the most outstanding season.

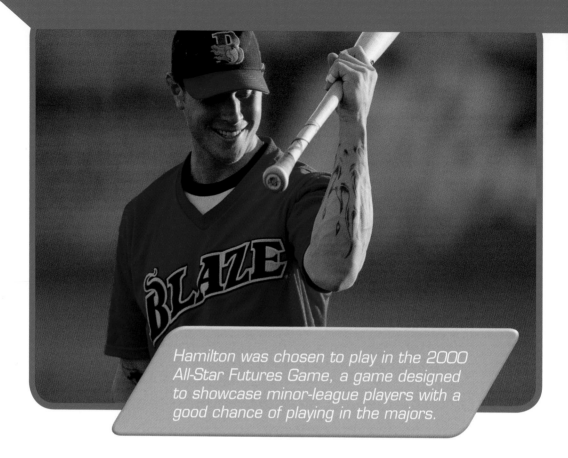

Hamilton was chosen to play in the 2000 All-Star Futures Game, a game designed to showcase minor-league players with a good chance of playing in the majors.

Hamilton did not play for the Devil Rays yet, but he played for one of their minor-league teams. He started with the Princeton Pirates, where he quickly proved himself to be one of the best players. Before the end of the season, the Devil Rays moved him to the next level, and he joined the Hudson Valley Renegades. Hamilton played for several different teams during his days in the minor leagues.

His parents quit their jobs and moved out of Raleigh so they could join him in every new town and watch him at every game. They even cooked his meals for him. *Baseball America* called Hamilton the game's top prospect in 2001. This meant he was the best player in the minors. All his life Hamilton had dreamed of playing in the majors. That dream now seemed so close.

When playing in the minor leagues, Hamilton started every game by leaning into the stands to give his mother a kiss on the cheek.

Crash

Josh Hamilton's life changed in February 2001 when he and his parents were in a bad car accident. A truck ran a red light and crashed into their car. Josh's mother was seriously **injured**. Josh suffered back injuries. His parents returned to Raleigh so that his mother could heal. Josh joined a new team in Orlando, Florida, but his back bothered him. He played only 23 games that season.

Without his parents around, Hamilton was on his own for the first time in his life. While too injured to play baseball, he needed something to take the place of sports in his life. Unfortunately, he started **abusing** drugs and alcohol.

A love of baseball runs in the Hamilton family. Josh Hamilton's parents met on a baseball diamond and were married six months later.

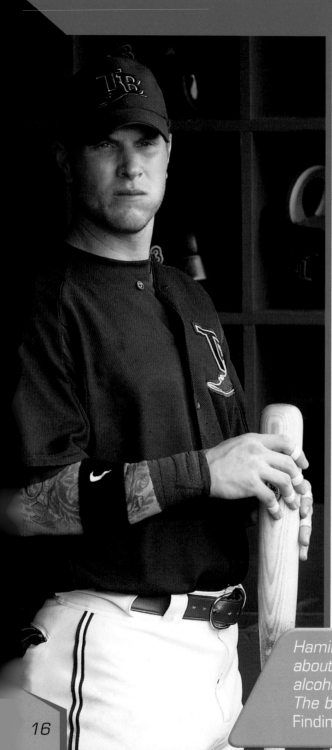

The Tampa Bay managers sent Hamilton to **rehab**, but recovering from addiction can be a long process. It is difficult to treat. It can take a long time for a person to be able to stop abusing drugs and alcohol. Hamilton returned to the baseball diamond that year, but injuries forced him back off the field. He then returned to drinking and abusing drugs.

Hamilton wrote an autobiography about his struggles with drugs and alcohol and returning to baseball. The book is called Beyond Belief: Finding the Strength to Come Back.

In 2003, when Hamilton kept failing drug tests, he had to stop playing baseball altogether. He eventually stopped taking the drug tests and was kicked out of Major League Baseball. It looked like he would never play again. More importantly, his addiction to drugs and alcohol was putting his life in danger.

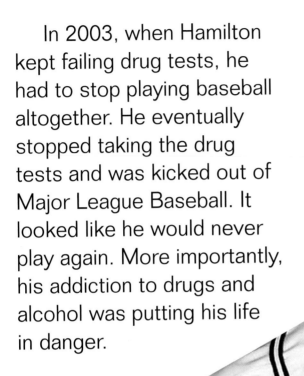

On February 18, 2004, Josh Hamilton was suspended for breaking Major League Baseball's substance-abuse rules. This meant that he was not allowed to play.

The Winning Inning

Hamilton was famous, so his struggles with addiction were in the news. A businessman named Mike Chadwick got in touch with him. Chadwick had been through a long battle with drug and alcohol addiction. He believed he could help Hamilton turn his life around. Hamilton then met Chadwick's daughter Katie, and the two fell in love.

Josh Hamilton married Katie Chadwick in 2004. It looked like he was finally clean, but then he **relapsed**, or fell back into addiction. His parents had given the couple money for a house, but Josh spent much of that money on drugs instead. Not even the birth of his daughter kept Josh from abusing drugs and alcohol. Katie made Josh move out until he got clean. He moved in with his grandmother. He had no money and nowhere else to go. Josh promised his grandmother he would beat his addiction.

Josh Hamilton's wife, Katie, did not see him play baseball until two years after they were married.

Here Josh Hamilton's family joins him in the 2008 MLB All-Star Game Red Carpet Show, a parade in New York City.

Another businessman and baseball fan reached out to help Hamilton. Roy Silver ran an organization called the Winning Inning. It was a baseball training school. Silver believed he could help Hamilton and invited him to work at the Winning Inning. Hamilton cleaned the restrooms and took care of the field. When he was finished with his jobs, he practiced playing baseball.

Josh Hamilton has never tried to hide his struggles with drugs and alcohol. He has made public apologies for his relapses.

All-Star Facts

Katie Hamilton stayed married to Josh through all his struggles. Katie has a daughter, Julia, from a previous relationship, and together she and Josh have three daughters, Sierra, Michaela, and Stella.

Most Valuable Player

The Cincinnati Reds decided to take a chance on Hamilton. He walked onto the field for his first Major League game on April 2, 2007, and the crowd went wild. Hamilton played well for the Reds in 2007, but the team struggled. They needed good pitchers more than they needed Hamilton's bat. They traded him to the Texas Rangers.

Here Hamilton watched from the bench on July 4, 2007, as the Cincinnati Reds played the San Francisco Giants. The Giants beat the Reds, 9–5.

Hamilton became the Rangers' star hitter in 2008. He was an easy pick for the All-Star Game. This is a special game that happens every season. Fans vote for the best players at each position. One of the most exciting parts of the All-Star weekend celebration is the Home Run Derby. This is simply a home run contest. Hamilton belted home run after home run in his first Home Run Derby and came in second place. He finished the 2008 season leading the American League with 130 **runs batted in**, or RBIs.

Hamilton was out for several weeks during the 2009 season to heal a bruised rib cage and to get surgery to repair a tear in his stomach muscle.

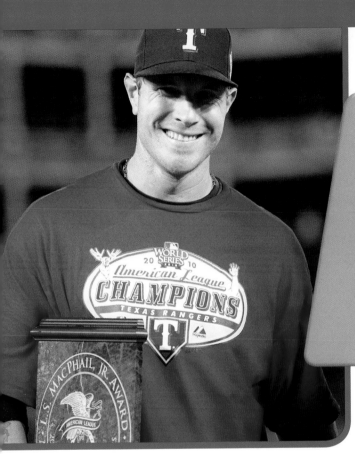

The 2009 season was more difficult. Hamilton got drunk at a bar in Arizona. He apologized to fans and passed a drug test two days later. Hamilton bounced back in 2010 with one of the best seasons in baseball history. He finished the season with 100 RBIs, 32 home runs, and an excellent **batting average** of .359. Baseball writers and experts chose him as the American League Most Valuable Player, or MVP.

Giving Back

Hamilton was chosen to appear in the 2012 All-Star Game. He received 11,073,744 votes, the highest number of fan votes received by any player in the history of the game.

Some might think that Hamilton's history of drug abuse makes him a poor **role model**. However, he is a role model for people struggling with addictions. Hamilton knows that helping others is more important than baseball.

Hamilton created an organization called the FourTwelve Foundation. It raises money to fight drug abuse and **poverty** and help people all over the world.

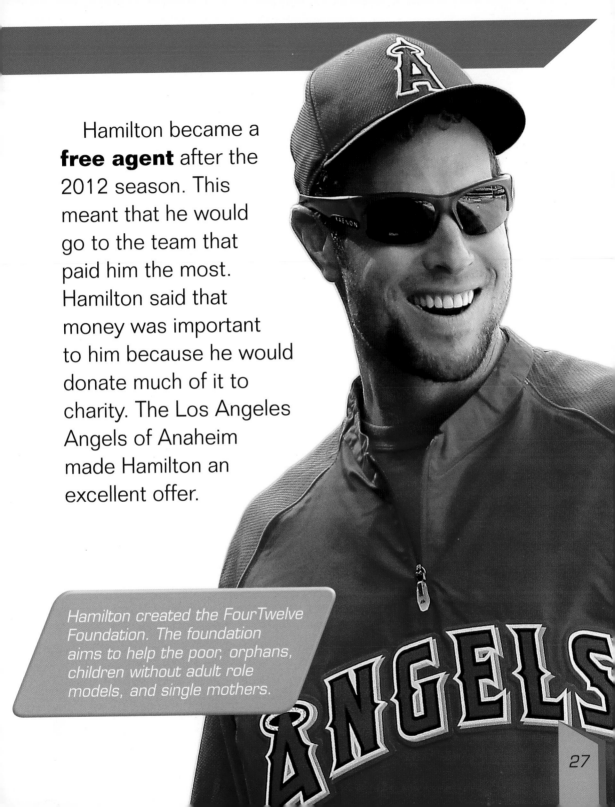

Hamilton became a **free agent** after the 2012 season. This meant that he would go to the team that paid him the most. Hamilton said that money was important to him because he would donate much of it to charity. The Los Angeles Angels of Anaheim made Hamilton an excellent offer.

Hamilton created the FourTwelve Foundation. The foundation aims to help the poor, orphans, children without adult role models, and single mothers.

The Natural

Hamilton's life might seem like a movie. He was a young star eager to make his dreams come true. Then he nearly lost everything. He worked hard to beat his addiction and to return to the world of baseball. Today, he is one of the best hitters in the game. Some fans give Hamilton the nickname Roy Hobbs after the hero from the film *The Natural*. Hamilton's story mirrors the story of Hobbs. It is important, though, to remember that Hamilton's story happened in real life. The people he helps are also real. This is what makes Hamilton's life much better than a movie.

In December 2012, Josh Hamilton agreed to a five-year, $125 million contract with the Los Angeles Angels of Anaheim.

Stat Sheet

Team: Los Angeles Angels of Anaheim
Position: Outfielder
Bats: Left
Throws: Left
Number: 32
Born: May 21, 1981
Height: 6 feet 4 inches (1.9 m)
Weight: 225 pounds (102 kg)

Season	Team	Batting Average	RBIs	Home Runs
2007	Cincinnati Reds	.292	47	19
2008	Texas Rangers	.304	130	32
2009	Texas Rangers	.268	54	10
2010	Texas Rangers	.359	100	32
2011	Texas Rangers	.398	94	25
2012	Texas Rangers	.285	128	43

Glossary

abusing (uh-BYOOZ-ing) Treating or using something in a harmful way.

addiction (uh-DIK-shun) A bad habit that is hard to break.

alcohol (AL-kuh-hol) A liquid, such as beer or wine, that can make a person lose control or get drunk.

batting average (BA-ting A-veh-rij) A number that measures how good a hitter is. It is the number of hits divided by at bats.

drafted (DRAFT-ed) Picked for a special purpose.

free agent (FREE AY-jent) A player who is not signed with a team and who can sign with whichever team offers him the best contract.

injured (IN-jurd) Harmed or hurt.

outfield (OWT-feeld) The part of a baseball field that is far away from home plate.

poverty (PAH-ver-tee) The state of being poor.

rehab (REE-hab) Making someone healthy again by helping him or her stop abusing drugs or alcohol.

relapsed (REE-lapst) To have gone back to abusing drugs or alcohol.

role model (ROHL MAH-dul) A person other people want to be like, a hero.

runs batted in (RUNZ BAT-ed IN) When a player's at bat results in runs being scored, usually abbreviated RBIs.

Index

A
addiction(s), 5,
    16–17, 19, 26, 29
alcohol, 5, 14,
    16–17, 19
athletes, 6, 11

B
Baseball America, 9,
    13
batting average, 25,
    30

C
career, 11

D
drugs, 5, 14, 16–17,
    19

F
fan(s), 6, 20, 24–25,
    29

H
high school, 5, 8–9
hitter(s), 5, 8, 24, 29

M
Major League
    Baseball, 5, 11,
    17

O
outfield, 8

P
parents, 6, 13–14,
    19

pitch, 9
Player of the Year, 9
poverty, 26

R
Raleigh, North
    Carolina, 6,
    13–14
rehab, 16
role model, 26
runs batted in
    (RBIs), 24–25, 30

S
scouts, 11
star(s), 5, 9, 29

T
teammates, 8

Websites

Due to the changing nature of Internet links, PowerKids Press has developed an online list of websites related to the subject of this book. This site is updated regularly. Please use this link to access the list: www.powerkidslinks.com/asp/hamil/